CW01072868

Gospel for dog lovers

Susan Sayers

With thanks to Rags
for his doggy ministry

kevin
mayhew

God's faithfulness is like
regular, dependable
feeding, and daylight
following darkness.

'Follow me' invites the same
kind of response as the
W-A-L-K word.

Be dogged in prayer -
it's that 'hanging on to
a bone' quality.

Enjoying and praising God's creation is like investigating every smell and scuffle with a grin at one end and a thrashing tail at the other.

Adoration. You've seen it in your dog's eyes. Now gaze at God like that.

Be attentive to God's voice -
like the way a can opener
is heard from the bottom
of the garden.

Praying is like being with your owner on the beach, when they've got plenty of time to throw your stick as often as you collect it and drop it damply at their feet.

Sorting out sin is as unattractive and as necessary as bathtime after rolling in a cowpat.

Guilt from unhealed sin feels like when you've been shut out of the kitchen, and the door won't open however much you hurl yourself at it.

Forgiveness and healed sin
is like being let off the
lead so you're free and
accepted, trusted
and happy.

The wolf will live with the lamb, the leopard will lie down with the goat, the calf and the lion and the yearling together, and a little child will lead them. Isaiah 11:6

Like a puppy on a lead,
we are so often more
interested in all the other
directions than the one God
is wanting to lead us in.

There are times we won't
budge either, and just sit
firmly on the pavement,
refusing to move.

Like shepherd and sheepdog working as a team, we are invited to work together with God.

'Lord, even the dogs eat
the crumbs that fall
from their master's table.'
Then Jesus answered her,
'Woman, great is your faith!
Let it be done for you as
you wish.' And her daughter
was healed instantly.
Matthew 15:27-28

Real partnership with God has to involve us in a working, relationship of trust and obedience.

Dogs aren't the only ones who need obedience and training classes.

There are times when God gives us the 'sit' and 'stay' commands, and times when it's 'come!' or 'leave!' Acting on the call we hear takes lots of practice and self-discipline.

Drink wholeheartedly
of God's love - like a dog
laps water on a hot day
after a long walk.

We need to learn that 'walking to heel' trick. Not rushing ahead of God, not lagging behind, but keeping close and attentive.

Like a dog, we learn
to recognise our
master's voice.

The moon marks off the seasons, and the sun knows when to go down. You bring darkness, it becomes night, and all the beasts of the forest prowl. The lions roar for their prey and seek their food from God. The sun rises, and they steal away; they return and lie down in their dens.

Psalm 104:19-22

God our Keeper knows
what we need to stay
healthy and strong -
spiritually as well as
mentally and physically.

When you catch sight of
God in the distance, run
flat out towards him,
single-minded and
expectant. You are his
and he is yours.

Sniff out the marks of
God's presence, dig with
abandon for his treasure,
guard bravely against evil
and wait on his command.

Get your teeth into
whatever is good and
loving, right, just and true,
and hang on to it for dear
life. Let nothing and no one
take it from you.

Dogs can only be themselves.
Let God free you up to be
yourself. It's the you he
already knows and loves.

Like guide dogs, we may
be asked to help one
another to see.

Faithful love means
sometimes barking out a
warning of danger. And
sometimes those in danger
don't want to hear.

Pursue righteousness, godliness, faith, love, endurance, gentleness. Fight the good fight of the faith; take hold of eternal life . . .

1 Timothy 6:11-12

First published in 2003 by
KEVIN MAYHEW LTD
Buxhall Stowmarket
Suffolk IP14 3BW
E-mail: info@kevinmayhewltd.com

9 8 7 6 5 4 3 2 1 0

ISBN 1 84417 005 5
Catalogue No 1500557

Designed by Angela Selfe
Edited by Katherine Laidler
Printed and bound in China